LIFE
with
MAXIE

DIANE REHM

PHOTOGRAPHS BY CINDY BERTAUT

GIBBS SMITH
TO ENRICH AND INSPIRE HUMANKIND

*To those who love and care
for dogs everywhere.*

First Edition
14 13 12 11 10 5 4 3 2 1

Published by
Gibbs Smith
P.O. Box 667
Layton, Utah 84041

1.800.835.4993 orders
www.gibbs-smith.com

Designed by Debra McQuiston
Printed and bound in China
Gibbs Smith books are printed on either recycled, 100% post-consumer waste,
FSC-certified papers or on paper produced from a 100% certified sustainable forest/
controlled wood source.

Library of Congress Cataloging-in-Publication Data

Rehm, Diane.
  Life with Maxie / Diane Rehm ; photographs by Cindy Bertaut. — 1st ed.
     p. cm.
  ISBN-13: 978-1-4236-1627-6
  ISBN-10: 1-4236-1627-8
  1. Chihuahua (Dog breed)—United States. 2. Rehm, Diane. 3. Human-animal
relationships—United States. 4. Chihuahua (Dog breed)—United States—Pictorial
works. 5. Rehm, Diane—Pictorial works. 6. Women radio talk show hosts—United
States—Biography. 7. Radio talk show hosts—United States—Biography. I. Title.
  SF429.C45R44 2010
  636.76—dc22
                                                      2010005867

CONTENTS

LONGING

for

MAXIE

I fell in love with Maxie, my long-haired Chihuahua, long before I met him. In the Dallas International Airport in the fall of 2002, one of Maxie's distant relatives was lying on his back, stretched out in his owner's lap, having his tummy rubbed. He was brown and white, with soft, silky long hair, a beautiful apple head, and gorgeous eyes, angelic in his pose of utter contentment. John and I were touring for our book about marriage, *Toward Commitment.* It was my first encounter with a long-haired Chihuahua, and I would not forget it.

In my lifetime, there have been several dogs I've loved. During my childhood, there were three: Patsy, a brown and white terrier; Skippy, an all-black terrier; and finally, Caramel, a blonde Cocker Spaniel. They were all dear to me, creatures who loved without expectation. They were part of my growing up, true friends in whom I could confide my greatest joys and worst fears. As I walked each of these dogs, before and after school, I would talk with them about what had happened during the day, my teachers, my friends, my parents, and all the worries I as a young girl had.

When John and I married, and after the children had reached the ages of about six and nine, we brought into our home a purebred long-haired Dachshund, Katinka, a beautiful red-haired female who became a loving family companion for fifteen years. Our daughter, Jennie, was learning to ride horses at the time. So, with the help of her father, she created a system of hurdles over which she trained Tinka to jump. It was always a delight to see Tinka racing around the garden, jumping hurdles at Jennie's command.

Tinka was bred once, giving birth to a gorgeous litter of seven puppies. They arrived in our kitchen at two o'clock on a summer morning, with our entire family attending the mother. The puppies went to happy new owners quickly, all of whom reported on their good health and behavior.

But Tinka was not the only creature in the house. There were also two cats. Cricket was a nearly-dead stray our daughter adopted on one of our beach vacations and lovingly nursed back to health. She provided a number of our friends with adorable kittens. Also, there was Jibne (the Arabic word for "cheese"), who had been a gift from a friend. Both looked askance when Tinka first arrived. As time went on, however, they grudgingly accepted one another. Each knew where his or her feeding bowl was placed in the kitchen, and all waited patiently when it was time for meals.

Eventually, all of our pets reached old age and passed away, the children went off to school, and John and I were on our own. During those years I was so intensely involved in my work as a radio host for WAMU/NPR that the lack of a pet did not trouble me. From time to time, we talked about eventually owning another dog, but only casually. John's standard comment was, "When you retire." And, for the most part, I agreed. However, when I saw that beautiful creature at the Dallas Airport, all of my pet-longings began to bubble up once more.

I confess Chihuahuas of the short-haired variety had never particularly appealed to me prior to this meeting. But I was bowled over by this dog, so much so that I walked over to speak with the owner and sit beside her as she stroked him. I was immediately

enthralled with the dog's apparent intelligence, sensitivity, and beauty, which came through clearly in his eyes. His coat was unbelievably silky to the touch. I've always loved dogs, but for reasons hard to explain, this one really grabbed my heart.

I spent some time talking with the owner about the breed. She explained there were relatively few in this country, and that, should I be interested, we could be in touch by email and she would help me find a breeder. I put all of this into the back of my mind and walked away, but it was hard to take my eyes, and my memory, away from that dog.

Nearly a year after the encounter in Dallas, on a warm lazy Sunday morning in August of 2003, while John and I were enjoying a restful at-home vacation, I began to scan the newspaper ads for long-haired Chihuahuas. I had been in touch by email with the woman I'd met at the airport, but there had been no leads on breeders in the area. I cannot fully explain what it was that, finally, on that very morning, made me decide that *now* was the time to search. Perhaps it was just that I looked out into the garden and felt a yearning to see a little dog playing in the sunshine.

My husband saw me studying the want ads and asked what I was looking for. When I told him what I was doing, he asked why, since he felt we had an agreement not to get a dog until I retired. "I'm just looking," I said.

But there it was, as though miraculously placed there just for me: an ad for an all-black long-haired Chihuahua. Without a word to John, I put down the newspaper, went to the phone and dialed the number in the ad. "Yes," said the woman at the other end of the line. "I do have a purebred long-haired Chihuahua, twelve weeks old. If you'd like, I can show you the puppy today."

So, with my reluctant husband at my side, annoyed with me and muttering to himself about our earlier agreement, off we drove to meet the lady with the dog.

"I just want to look," I said.

"I'll bet," said John.

In silence, we drove an hour to her office in Frederick, Maryland. When we walked in, my eyes immediately fell to the floor where *two* adorable little twelve-week-old puppies, one male, one female, were happily romping. Two tiny, fuzzy black creatures, playing with each other, one a little more assertive than the other. I sat down on the floor to gaze at them, watching them nuzzle and tumble over each other. Touching each of them, I remarked to the owner that their fur seemed so minimal, like short baby hair, and extremely unlike the beautiful long-haired dog I'd seen in Dallas. She assured me that the fuzz would turn into a handsome and silky coat before long.

As I gazed at these tiny creatures, petting each one, holding each one, I cried out, "I want them both!"

"What? You're out of your mind!" John hollered. "We can't possibly take two puppies. And besides, you promised you'd wait."

And he was absolutely right. I had agreed to wait. But here were these babies, a brother and a sister, and I could not imagine separating them. I just kept thinking they'd be so happy together, and *we'd* be so happy watching them. At that moment, all of my repressed longings burst out loud and clear. Why? Perhaps it was the realization that our children were gone from our home forever, leading their own productive lives. Perhaps there was a yearning on my part to replace our children. Our pets had all lived long and lovely lives, but they, too, were gone. Perhaps I just *needed* a creature to *need me.* Out loud, I said, "I know I agreed to wait, but I'm longing for a puppy now."

Here we were, two seemingly mature adults who'd written a successful book on marriage, who'd toured the country lecturing and offering guidance to others as to how *they* could deal with their differences, and here *we* were behaving like two stubborn children. The owner looked aghast. She said with some discomfort, "I can see you two have some things to talk about."

John and I excused ourselves and went out on the porch. John said angrily, "You promised me you'd wait until after you'd retired!"

"I know I said that awhile back, but I really have no idea when I'll retire. It could be *years* from now. And besides," I said, "*you've* retired. *You* would be there with a dog. I have no idea when *I'll* retire, and I'm truly longing for a dog now. And they're both so beautiful!"

But John would not budge. Looking at the anger reflected in his face and body language, I knew it would be a losing battle if I continued to pursue with him the idea of bringing two puppies into our lives.

Of course, I was hurt, angry, and embarrassed that this had erupted into such a loud and personal disagreement in front of the puppies' owner. But I was also terribly disappointed. I had, perhaps foolishly, hoped that seeing the pups would change John's attitude, and that he would be as enthusiastic as I about having a new pet once he saw the puppy. But clearly, at that moment, it was not to be.

So after the unproductive exchange outdoors, we walked back into the owner's office in silence. I was in tears, and said to her, my voice shaking, "I'm sorry to have brought you all the way here, but I'm afraid my husband is just not ready for a dog." Then, to my utter and absolute amazement, John quickly spoke up. "Oh, no," he said. "I'll take *one* of the pups. And I think we should take the little boy." Oh, sweet sigh of relief! I looked at him with my mouth wide open, then laughed and threw my arms around him, saying, "Thank you, sweetheart." At that moment, and after our heated exchange on the porch, I think he had finally realized just how much I wanted a little dog and decided it was too important an issue to deny me. I also believe he saw how absolutely charming the pup was. The male was the more playful and outgoing. He came right up to us and licked our fingers, wagging his tail. However much John didn't want to admit it, he too thought the puppy was adorable. So, in the end, a compromise. One little puppy, a boy, came home with us.

Why had the moment finally arrived when I knew I not only wanted, but *needed,* a puppy? I believe that for that entire year I'd been secretly longing for the dog in the Dallas airport, without allowing myself to voice that desire. Yet somehow I knew the time was right: there were no other creatures to care for or to offer me the kind of uncompromising love I'd felt from other dogs or cats we'd had in the past. I needed a creature who accepted me totally, to whom

I could speak in funny baby-like words, who would, in my imagination, laugh with me at my own silliness, who would play on the floor with me, lick my face, and tickle my chin. And John, now retired, would also benefit from having a creature to care for in the home while I went about my professional life. The house was too quiet, too calm, without the kind of small noises animals make or the playfulness they inject. Of course, there was also my dream: to have a little dog to take to the office with me on occasion, to sit with me at my desk, to go into the studio with me, to be a quiet and comforting companion.

SMART PUP

Driving home, delighted with our ability to ultimately reach a quiet peace, and with a tiny black pup in my lap, John suggested that since he was a dog of Mexican origin, with the rounded apple head and large eyes, he should be given a name appropriate to the breed. "Maximilian," he said. "Nineteenth-century emperor of Mexico."

"Perfect," I said. "And we'll call him Maxie!"

So Maxie moved into our home and into a large fenced garden filled with beautifully tended flowers.

We immediately took him outside, placed him in the grass (which was tall enough to nearly cover him), and walked around the garden. Right away, he peed. Smart pup, I thought. He'll get the order of things quickly.

And my instinct was right. He was house-trained easily. We were both at home for the next few weeks and could put him outdoors every half hour. I loved sitting in the grass playing with him. Maxie was an incredibly responsive puppy, watching every move we made. When I worked in the garden, he would play for a time and then sit next to me. If neither of us was outside, he would sit on the stoop leading from the kitchen, basking in the sunshine. Indoors, we had purchased a crate in which he happily dwelled, except for times out to eat and to play. Within a very short time, he could be trusted throughout the kitchen, and then the house and even on our bed overnight. We realized very soon that he could sleep through the night without an accident. As soon as one of us rose early in the morning, we'd put him out in the backyard to relieve himself. His internal discipline was remarkable.

However, there was one small problem we noted shortly after Maxie came to live with us. Out in the garden and in the house, he could run like the wind when excited. But he walked with a slight limp in his right leg. Since we had no intention of turning Maxie into a show dog, the limp didn't bother us at all, but I wondered whether it was uncomfortable for him. On our very first visit to the vet, we were told that Maxie had what she called a "short shoulder," which created the limp but clearly did not impede his running.

I've often wondered whether he was born with the problem and we just hadn't noticed it early on, or whether an event that occurred shortly after we brought Maxie home might have contributed to it, and to even other, more serious, behavioral difficulties that followed.

A TINY
barking
MACHINE

The incident occurred when dear friends came to visit and brought with them two young children, each of whom was longing to hold the sweet-smelling new puppy. Alas, Maxie was such a wiggly little creature that he fell from one child's arms onto a wooden floor, hitting his head and yelping, running off and away from all of us to hide under a chair. Might that fall have injured his leg, and possibly so frightened Maxie that it affected his entire personality? Who can know.

But I do wonder, because shortly thereafter,

Maxie began growling at the sight of strangers, barking fiercely at anyone who came to the door, whether the mailman or the little girl across the street. It was as though he became another dog, no longer a funny, friendly pup, happy to be held and played with. With just two exceptions, John and I were the only people who could hold him and with whom he was at ease. He even began to snap at anyone who tried to pet him! But because he was so adorable looking, *everyone* wanted to pet him.

On his second visit, the veterinarian had to muzzle him just for a routine exam. Even worse, if I were in bed with Maxie by my side and John approached, Maxie would begin growling, even fiercely at times. Eventually he would settle down, but we both became increasingly concerned that this was a pup that would have to be watched every minute when other people were around.

Of the two others in Maxie's immediate circle of

acceptable friends, one was our son, David. Shortly after Maxie came to live with us, John and I had to go out of town. David and his wife, Nancy, who live in Gettysburg, agreed to come down to Washington to stay the night and care for Maxie. In fact, that night David slept on the floor in the kitchen with Maxie so he wouldn't feel lonely. From that moment on, the two became real pals. Now when David visits or we go to Gettysburg, Maxie jumps with joy right into David's lap, wagging his tail, licking his face, clearly delighted to see his good friend.

The other person Maxie adored was our neighbor across the street, Thea Clarke. Thea is a young woman slightly older than our son, who, in earlier years, had been a babysitter for both of our children. Maxie seemed to understand that Thea was "one of the family," someone I saw frequently outdoors and in our home. At first, Maxie would sit in my lap if Thea and I were in the living room together. But before long he would get down and move toward Thea's chair. At first tentatively, and later enthusiastically, Maxie went happily into her arms.

Both David and Thea talked to Maxie using soft, gentle voices. Both waited for Maxie to approach them. And both got down on the floor with him. I do wonder how such tiny dogs feel about the huge humans towering above them. They must, at some level, be terrified. But at some point, they learn to trust that they will not be harmed.

Maxie's life at our home was little short of idyllic. He had the house to himself and a beautiful garden in which to run and play or to sit beside me as I worked in the flowerbeds. Occasionally he would run off to chase a teasing squirrel or bark at a nearby bird.

And there was a huge black Labrador who lived on the other side of the fence, with whom Maxie would run up and down, barking and racing back and forth. Good exercise for both!

Late that first summer, when Maxie was just three months old, we were invited down to Bethany Beach to the home of friends we'd known for many years. It was agreed we would bring Maxie with us. Our host had her own dog, a lovely and gentle yellow Lab named Daisy. The host felt, as did I, that the two would get along together quite easily. Alas, that didn't happen. Poor Daisy was totally intimidated by Maxie, who barked and nipped at her feet. Since Maxie was too small to climb stairs, Daisy decided the better part of wisdom was to seek refuge on the upstairs landing, out of reach of this tiny barking, nipping machine.

To our horror, not only did Maxie nip at Daisy, he actually bit our host's finger, drawing blood. It was extremely embarrassing and created a greater concern for us that Maxie simply could or would not behave well outside his own domain. Though our hosts were kind, it was clear they were unhappy with Maxie's behavior.

There was a wonderfully amusing moment, however. The first time we took Maxie out on the beach for a walk we realized just how tiny he was. He lifted his leg to pee, and the wind blew him over! We've always laughed about that. He was happy to run and play in the sand, as long as he could stand up and not get caught by an ocean wave!

Later that summer, we went on vacation to a resort that did not allow dogs. Unfortunately Maxie then had to have his very first experience with a kennel. We went out to visit the facility, which had come highly recommended. It was for just one week. But sadly, for that one week, Maxie refused to eat and barely emerged from his individually fenced kennel with a run attached to it, which he came out of only to relieve himself. When we returned, I vowed I would never again place Maxie in a kennel, no matter for how brief a period.

STUBBORN
little
DOG

As fall arrived, I took joy in watching Maxie chasing floating leaves, perhaps regarding them as mysterious intruders. But he soon realized they represented no real threat and ultimately sat in the sunshine watching them fall. It was about this time that I decided it would be good to take Maxie for regular walks in the neighborhood, to give him a taste of the world outside his own garden. So I purchased a small harness and a leash and proceeded to carry him out our front door to the street and put him down, expecting him to move forward and follow my lead. No such luck. No budging, much less walking. And no amount of cajoling, pulling, or tempting with treats could get him to move. He just sat there! Now, I was really confused. Who'd ever heard of a dog that wouldn't walk? So, on that first day, I carried him back into the house and back out to the garden, wondering how we could get this project going. At first I speculated it was his "short shoulder" somehow preventing him from walking on a leash. But the more I thought about his ability to run like the wind inside the house and outside in the garden, the more I came to the conclusion that we had a stubborn little pup on our hands. Day after day I tried, using different tactics. I even asked his adored friend, Thea, to walk with us. No luck. He'd move for two steps, stop, sit down, and refuse to budge. What to do?

Answer? I bought him a stroller! A doggie stroller, in which he could either sit down at the bottom or put

his paws at the top and look over the rim. He seemed to have no objection to this, so that became our daily practice, strolling Maxie through the neighborhood. He looked adorable, with his little head popping up from time to time to see who or what was ahead. Of course, again, people wanted to pet him, but Maxie would have none of it, growling when a stranger came too close. Clearly, we were both enjoying fresh air, but I was the one getting the exercise, not Maxie!

Our walking/strolling days came to a close when the first winter snow arrived. Of course Maxie had to go outdoors, and he was curious about the white stuff. So he took one big leap and landed in a big drift, way taller than he. His size meant he was virtually buried up to his nose. John then shoveled out a path so that he could have a way to walk around the garden. I'd see his footprints everywhere in the snow. Later, when it turned to ice, he'd walk on top of it, occasionally falling a few inches before clambering up again.

Maxie and me at the studio.

LIFE HAS A
way of
CHANGING

When we first purchased our home back in 1967, I thought we'd be there forever. Even after the children left to create their own families, our house was just right for the two of us. We refurbished the entire interior of the house, remodeled the kitchen, created a beautiful patio, worked diligently to see the garden grow from an unkempt play yard to a magnificent flower-filled haven from the noise of the outside world, and we assumed we would continue to enjoy it. But life has a way of changing, and in our case, it changed a lot.

In 2004, John was diagnosed with Parkinson's Disease. Mild though it may have been at the time, we realized we could not be sure of what lay ahead, and that we would inevitably face changes, both in our ability to navigate a four-story house as well as to maintain it. At first, John resisted. He wanted to stay in our home. And so did I! After all, our children had grown up in this home. We loved our neighbors and the neighborhood. I cherished memories of John, David, Jennie and all the neighborhood kids playing soccer in the street, watching Jennie learn to ride a unicycle, seeing David and his dad throwing a ball back and forth, welcoming trick-or-treaters on Halloween, and having our beautiful daughter's wedding reception in our garden. Nevertheless, I knew the time had come. I began looking at condominiums soon after we received the diagnosis. Our children telephoned regularly to urge us to move to a safer environment without stairs to navigate, and to do it soon.

So I kept looking, though John continued to say he wouldn't move. But one incident, perhaps brought on by medication, convinced him and me that the time had come. At about 3 a.m. one late summer morning, John arose from his bed, walked in his sleep, opened wide both the front and back doors, and went back upstairs to sleep, with no memory of what he'd done. When I went down in the morning and found both doors open, I knew we had to have both a change in medication as well as a change of residence. Faced with the reality of what he'd done, and hearing his children and me plead with him, John finally said, "You're right. It's time to move."

Together, after nearly a year of searching, we eventually found the perfect apartment, complete with a gorgeous view of trees and lots of light. And the condo accepted small dogs. The real question was: would Maxie fit into a new way of living at a condo? After all, it would mean no more private garden. No more basking in the sunshine or chasing squirrels. No more running up and down the fence with the neighbor's black Lab. No more being by himself and just with us all day long. Instead, elevators, doormen, receptionists, other residents, and other dogs. I was worried. Would he behave? Would he bark? Would he snarl? Would he bite? Would he ever adjust?

During the four-month period when the apartment was being renovated, we brought Maxie over frequently, hoping that he would begin to feel comfortable in the new environment, despite the constant presence of workmen, loud noise, and strange smells. Though Maxie adored our contractor, John Baliles, and had known him since he was a puppy, we had absolutely no idea how long—or whether—his adjustment would take. We worried.

But happily, and eventually, it happened. His transition began slowly. Our condo is in an area surrounded by parks, so John and I were both able to take Maxie outdoors each day, which we began doing even before the move to acclimate him to the surrounding area.

We finally moved into our new home in March of 2008. Little by little, Maxie grew accustomed to the smells of the park, the trees, and the sidewalks, so that he finally agreed to be walked with on a leash. That still left the adjustment to the many people he encountered. We held him in our arms as we went up and down in the elevators, cautioning those who saw him to keep their distance. His resistance to other humans was as great—if not greater—than his reluctance to walk on a leash.

And then, a small miracle. One of the doormen in our condo, Nervo, began taking the time to bend down each day and speak softly to Maxie. He would put out his hand, palm up, urging Maxie to come forward with endearing gestures and words. Each time Maxie encountered Nervo, he would inch closer and closer, until *voíla!* One day he allowed Nervo to scratch him on the head. That tiny gesture signaled a huge breakthrough.

Small gestures led to bigger movements. Others, seeing Nervo successfully engaging the dog, began speaking to Maxie more softly and sweetly, commenting on what a beautiful and well-behaved little dog he was. They admired his shiny long black coat, his sweet face, good manners in the elevator, and the dipping of his head when people approached him. A clear transition had begun toward shedding his fear of strangers.

Maxie and Nervo.

COMPANIONSHIP
and
COMFORT

Now a year and a half later, at age six, Maxie accompanies me to my studio almost every day. Each morning as I prepare for the short car ride, he waits by the front door, knowing that because I have briefcase in hand, we're going to the office, and that when he gets there, treats will be awaiting him. During my mornings on the air, he's in the studio under the table with me or in my office under my desk. He greets guests with a wave of his plume-like tail and approaches them with his head down, assuming there'll be a sweet pat on the head. I know that I have only to look down on him, or he up at me, and I feel easier, more relaxed, and even more confident. Every now and then, as I am in mid-sentence about some extremely serious topic, he'll put his forepaws up to my lap, asking me to scratch his head, or even pleading to sit in my lap.

Our subject in 2009 was frequently Afghanistan, an extraordinarily difficult subject for me and for our listeners. There might be two guests in the studio and one on the phone, and my complete focus would be on the subject at hand. And yet, at a moment during those conversations, Maxie would poke his head up, looking at me in his own endearing way, and I would feel myself relaxing. I can recall one program in particular in which we discussed mental health among those serving in the U.S. military with Yochi Dreazen of the *Wall Street Journal* and Nancy Sherman, professor of philosophy at Georgetown University and author of a book titled *The Untold War: Inside the Hearts and Minds and Souls of our Soldiers.* The sadness of war and the loss of humanity that were part of that conversation struck me very hard, so much so that tears came to my eyes. Somehow Maxie must have sensed my sadness, because he put his front paws on my knees asking to be petted, but at the same time, perhaps, trying to comfort me. I know there are many stories of comfort dogs, helping people who are sick, in hospitals, or in nursing homes. But I wonder whether anyone else in the world has a comfort dog in a radio studio?

All of our guests seem delighted to see Maxie. I bring him into the studio in my arms, and there are invariably oohs and ahs and questions about Maxie's breed. When I put him down on the floor, people call to him, wanting to pet him. Some put their hands down for him to lick; others simply marvel that he is so well behaved in the studio. Maxie's preference is clearly toward women, especially those who gesture toward him softly and quietly. I urge everyone to ignore him and let him come to them. Even special treats don't tempt him—he's a very cautious pup. Dr. Patricia McConnell, professor of zoology at the University of Wisconsin and a certified animal behaviorist, brought along numerous treats for Maxie, to no avail. She finally put the treats on the tabletop in the studio and let her hand fall down by her side during our conversation on the air. Lo and behold, Maxie walked over to her and began rubbing his head against her hand. He had finally decided Dr. McConnell was safe. The same is true when guests come to our apartment. At parties large and small, we urge everyone to ignore Maxie, to let him come to them, and before long, he does.

Remarkably, there has been only one instance when he barked while we were on the air. It happened when Greg Mortenson, author of the bestselling book *Three Cups of Tea,* barged into the studio a half-hour late. Maxie, in his ever-protective mode, barked vigorously. In my effort to quiet him down, I said, "Maxie Rehm, hush! It's our guest!" Maxie continued to bark for a few seconds but then fortunately quieted down. Everybody in the whole world heard Maxie bark—including my colleagues at NPR, who razzed me about it afterwards. So indeed, my listeners now really know he's in the studio while I'm on the air.

When work is done, Maxie and I do errands together. Sometimes he's able to enter a card store or gift shop with me. My beauty salon welcomes small dogs, and when I say to Maxie, "Let's go see Mustafa," I am certain he knows we're going to get my hair done. As I go through these rituals, he sits on the floor or in a chair beside me. Even now, however, if he is sitting right next to me, he is in "guard mode" and will growl if he's approached. At grocery stores, where he is not permitted to come inside, he waits patiently for me in the car.

On our way home, we stop at what John and I call "Maxie Park," a sweet spread of lawn bordering community gardens across from our condominium. There he can once again be in the kind of soft, grassy environment he knew as a puppy, rolling, stretching, sniffing, but also seeing other dogs.

But sometimes I'm away. I travel to other cities to visit NPR stations around the country and am not always able to take him with me. When I am gone, Maxie sometimes hides from John under my desk in the opening we call "Maxie's Cave." There have been days when he's refused to come out for as much as fourteen or sixteen hours! Finally, out of necessity, he moves!

Our earlier sad experience with boarding Maxie at a kennel convinced us that we simply had to find a trustworthy and willing caretaker. Lo and behold, on a visit to our revered dermatologist, Dr. Carol McNeely, she volunteered her services along with those of her husband, Arnold Spitzen. They have long cared for the dogs of friends and neighbors of all types and sizes. And they have their own Max, a lovely friendly and gentle chocolate Lab.

So, in 2009, when we went on vacation to the Poconos with our children, there was no need to be on the phone with a shelter attendant each day to check on Maxie's status. I was getting emails and photos of Maxie relaxing on the bed, watching television, enjoying his meals, and thoroughly relishing the attention he was getting from his new caretakers, who have clearly become good friends of ours and Maxie's. In fact, while we cruised the Nile and traveled to Egypt and Jordan with NPR listeners, Maxie stayed with Arnie and Carol for a full three weeks! We feel extremely blessed to have found such good and caring friends.

Just a few weeks before we were due to leave on our trip to the Nile, however, I encountered a major problem that threw into doubt whether I would be able to travel at all. I had gone to a nearby department store to pick up a single item. It was a hot day, and I did not want Maxie to be in the car by himself for more than three minutes. So I rushed in, completed the transaction, and ran back to my car in the parking lot across the street from the store. Unfortunately, as I stepped off the curb, I caught the heel of my shoe in the hem of my slacks, and fell—splat—in the middle of the street, on my right side. When I tried to get up, I realized I was so badly injured I could not stand. Fortunately two women saw me fall and rushed to help me. They immediately suggested calling an ambulance, but I said this was not possible, that I had to drive home because my little dog was waiting for me in my car. They shouldered my weight and got me to my car, again urging me to let them call for help, which I refused. I managed to get into the car and call my husband, crying, telling him I'd hurt myself and would need to have a wheel-chair waiting for me at the front of our condo building. He heard the pain in my voice and begged me to go straight to the nearby emergency room but I said I just wanted to come home with Maxie and go to bed.

I cannot tell you how I managed to drive home, with Maxie huddling in my lap, but I knew I had to get there to make sure he was safely in the apartment. By the time I reached our building, John was at the door with Nervo, who had a wheelchair waiting for me. However, I realized I could not get out of the car and into the wheelchair without excruciating pain in my right leg. I finally understood that I had no choice but to go to the emergency room at a nearby hospital. So, while John took a bewildered Maxie upstairs to our apartment, Nervo helped me into the wheelchair to get around into the passenger side of the car. When John, who no longer drives, came back downstairs, Nervo got behind the wheel and drove us to the emergency room of the hospital. There we waited for seven hours, until an MRI finally revealed that I'd fractured my pelvis. At that point, luckily, I was admitted to the hospital.

There I stayed for nine days, the first five in full hospital care and the last four in the rehabilitation portion of the facility. Luckily, a fractured pelvis does not require surgery, but there is a great deal of discomfort before the healing process begins. Dogs are not allowed in the hospital itself, but they are permitted to visit when patients are in rehab, so long as they have all of the inoculations and vaccinations verified by their veterinarian. The day when that little dog came racing into my room, up onto my bed, and began licking my face and wagging his tail was a very happy one. It was a joyous reunion for me and one that I truly believe assisted in my speedy recovery. His presence allowed me to relax, to forget the

COMPANIONSHIP AND COMFORT

pain, to enjoy his warmth and his unconditional love, to laugh at his antics, his immediate nestling on my bed, right next to my fractured pelvis. He wanted me back at home with him, and he let me know that he would be there waiting for me.

Each day John would bring Maxie in to see me in the afternoon, and we would spend a few hours together, as he sat on my bed and I rubbed his tummy. Gradually, as I was able to use a walker, John would take him by the leash and we would walk up and down the halls of the rehab center, greeting other patients who would ooh and aah over him. In fact, I actually put him on the carrying tray attached to the walker, which stirred up quite a joyful commotion among nurses and patients as I wheeled him through the corridors.

I have no doubts about the spiritual and emotional therapy that pets offer. It is their complete comprehension of the fact that there is a problem that allows them to enter our hearts and transmit the caring energy we need for healing.

That healing energy continued once I returned to our home. Maxie came with John and my dear friend, the former Episcopal Bishop Jane Dixon, to pick me up at the hospital on my day of discharge. Jane, too, is totally smitten with her dog, a sweet Boston Terrier named Arthur. Jane feels as I do, that dogs emit that indescribable loving energy. They never hold back when someone they adore is in need.

Friends, of course, are the same way. Jane asked what I needed or wanted when we got back home. "A bowl of strawberry Jell-O," I said. And within an hour, there it was.

Oh, what joy it was to once again be in my own room with Maxie by my side. I spent a good deal of those first few days at home in bed, and when I was in bed, Maxie was right there with me.

Then we were back to our usual regime. I was able to get back on the air, totally mobile with first a walker and then a cane. When I walk with Maxie these days, he understands that I am not walking as quickly as I used to and matches his pace to mine. When I take Maxie to the office, he knows treats await him, and he greets each of the show's producers with an expectant eye, wondering who will give him the next treat. He enjoys coming into the studio with me, and either sits quietly under the studio table or goes to sleep at my feet. After the show is over, he and I go for a brief walk, I give him a snack, and then he sleeps under my desk while I continue the day's work. We do our errands and then head for home.

Maxie so enjoys our time out together that when I don't bring him to work with me—which is maybe one day a week—he will walk to the area between the living room and the library and he'll sprinkle about five drops. It happens *only* when I'm not there. It's clearly a protest. Poor John tries to follow him around, and once he even caught him in the act.

Usually, however, Maxie never has accidents. In fact, he has so much self-restraint that he once refused to relieve himself at all during a terrible snowstorm. On December 19, 2009, which happened to be the date of our fiftieth wedding anniversary, Washington experienced its worst blizzard in decades. The snow was at least two feet deep around our apartment, and the wind rattled our windows. Into this extraordinary maelstrom, John attempted to take Maxie outdoors. Not just once or twice, but for three entire days. Maxie refused to relieve himself, neither peeing nor pooping! I became so concerned I called our veterinarian. I was told by a young man who'd clearly answered similar questions many times that the dog would go when he had to go. And he did. I had really prepared myself to spot an accident or two within the apartment, but it never happened. When he finally relieved himself for the first time on a walk along a shoveled path, I whooped with relief!

In the evening, after John, Maxie and I have had our dinner and we've washed and dried the dishes, Maxie comes to me with a favorite toy in his mouth. He knows it's time for bed, and he's ready to go through our nightly ritual. So I fold down the bedspread, put all six of his small rubber toys on the bed, and then lift him up. I wash my face, brush my teeth, put on my nightgown, and then as Maxie waits expectantly at the corner of the bed I bring him a glass of water to drink.

I like to read before I go to sleep. It's the one time I have to be able to read for pure pleasure. Sometimes that's okay with Maxie and sometimes it's not. If he's impatient and wants me to rub his tummy right away, he'll plant himself on my stomach and bat at my book with his paw. Depending on how interesting the book is, I may give in, or I may urge him to be patient. But finally, as I turn out the light after reading for perhaps half an hour, Maxie snuggles against me, a signal to both of us that all is well.

MAXIE'S PRESENCE

Maxie has changed. So have I. In ways I could not have imagined, his presence calms my soul. I am cheered by his nearness. I have only to glance at him or touch him or see his eyes and I am moved almost to tears. This little creature has brought me a kind of inner peace I could not have imagined for myself. The same is true for my husband, who, after his initial reluctance to take on a new pet prior to my retirement, enjoys his retirement in the company of Maxie.

Maxie's presence has even made our marriage stronger. John says having Maxie has made marriage easier. I think that because we both love Maxie so much, that kind of relationship that each of us has for Maxie expands to our relationship with each other. He's so dependent and so vulnerable that his love for us radiates, and our love for him sort of translates into our affection for one another. He has nourished our spirits.

Maxie has made me a far more patient person. The fact that he has undergone such a transition has helped me to understand that not only can creatures be transformed but people can be transformed as well. He has such sweetness that he makes me feel sweet. He makes me be kinder to everybody around me. John and I are better people because of Maxie. There's no question of it.